# THE BRIEF HISTORY OF BUDHA DAL

## FROM THE ESTABLISHMENT OF AKAL SENA TO THE CREATION OF BUDHA DAL

## ISHWAR SINGH

Copyright © Ishwar Singh
All Rights Reserved.

This book has been published with all efforts taken to make the material error-free after the consent of the author. However, the author and the publisher do not assume and hereby disclaim any liability to any party for any loss, damage, or disruption caused by errors or omissions, whether such errors or omissions result from negligence, accident, or any other cause.

While every effort has been made to avoid any mistake or omission, this publication is being sold on the condition and understanding that neither the author nor the publishers or printers would be liable in any manner to any person by reason of any mistake or omission in this publication or for any action taken or omitted to be taken or advice rendered or accepted on the basis of this work. For any defect in printing or binding the publishers will be liable only to replace the defective copy by another copy of this work then available.

I am dedicating this book to the unsung heroes of Sikh history.

# Contents

# Foreword

Ishwar Singh have more than ten years of experience in writing story books, sakhis of devotional saints and in research activities. He is a tremendous writer. He is doing excellent job by publishing about **The Brief History of Budha Dal.** He had shown very keen interest in the field of **historical resources** and other cultural issues.

He is also a very excellent teacher and also having deep knowledge about the social science issues. I have always seen him working very hard for his various books. He just want to express about the Indian culture to our new generations in a simple and brief manner. I wish him all the very best for his new book.

Birinder Pal Kaur

# Preface

This book elaborates the brief history of Budha Dal. Budha Dal is such an organisation in the Sikh history which had faced very hard times and fought various wars. I am publishing this content for my students who are unaware about the various Sikh organisations and unsung warriors. This is just an effort to spread this brief information among new generations.

# Acknowledgements

*I'm eternally grateful to my father Pal Singh, who took in an extra mouth to feed when he didn't have to. He taught me discipline, tough love, manners, respect, and so much more that has helped me succeed in life. I truly have no idea where I'd be if he hadn't given me a roof over my head whom I desperately needed at that age.*

*To my father-in-law Narinder Singh for their moral support during the up and downs in my life. He taught me how to live positive even in the worst situations by sharing his personal experiances. He is the man who suggest me to write a book in your life because it will be your book by which you will be remembered in future.*

*To Dr. Davinder Singh, who never saw my age, my race, or my lack of formal education. He just saw a kid hungry to learn, hungry to grow, and hungry to succeed in teaching. He never stopped me; he only encouraged me.*

# 1

# The Brief History of Budha Dal

The lineage of the Budha Dal traces back to the creation of the Akal Sena at the time of Sri Guru Hargobind Sahib Ji. Baba Budha Ji is considered one of the foremost Sikhs within the tradition, they were one of Sri Guru Nanak Dev Ji's closest disciples and served the first six Sikh Guru's. When Baba Budha Ji arrived at Gwallior fort, accompanied by Sikh warriors perched on horseback to greet the Sixth Guru, Sri Guru Hargobind Sahib was greatly pleased and granted the following boon;

When Sri Guru Gobind Singh Ji sent the Khalsa Panth with Baba Banda Singh Bahadur to Punjab form Nander, Baba Binod Singh was elected as the Jathedar of the Dal Khalsa, Khalsa army. Baba Binod Singh was of the seventh generation of Sri Guru Angad Dev Ji's family (second Sikh Guru), and had actively served Sri Guru Gobind Singh Ji. When differences arose between the Nihang Singhs loyal to Sri Guru Gobind Singh Ji and those Sikhs loyal to Baba Banda Bahadur, the Nihang Singhs lead by Baba Binod

Singh departed company with the others in order to keep alive the true traditions of the Khalsa. They became known as the Tat (true) Khalsa whereas the group loyal to Baba Banda Bahadur were known as the Bandai Khalsa. With the martyrdom of Baba Banda Singh Bahadur, the Khalsa was soon united again. After Baba Binod Singh, the humble and wise Baba Darbara Singh lead the Khalsa Panth. It was when Nawab Kapoor Singh assumed leadership of the Khalsa that the lineage of the Sikhs who actively served the Guru's were formally institutionalised as Budha Dal.

It is noteworthy that the Budha Dal still retains the original Nishan Sahib (battle standards) from some of these key historical events as a sign of their continuous Guru ordained lineage. These include a Nishan Sahib from Baba Budha Ji's trip to Gwallior and the Budha Dal Nishan sahib from the period of Navab Kapur Singh.

The Budha Dal served as the fifth mobile throne (Panjwan Takht) of the Sikhs. Akaal Takht, Patna Sahib, Kesgarh Sahib and Hazoor Sahib are the four stationary Takht Sahibs. For their maintenance was the Chalda Vaheer – moving encampment who would spend all their time moving from one historical shrine to another ensuring that those appointed to do so were properly performing duties at their entrusted Gurdwara Sahibs. Even today Budha Dal consists of a stationary unit and a Chalda Vaheer who roam around India spreading the message of the Sikh faith and visiting the historic shrines of the Guru, many of which still remain under the supervision of the Budha Dal.

The supreme leadership of the Budha Dal was greater evident at the time of Akali Phula Singh who, even during the reign of Maharaj Runjeet Singh of the Sikh Kingdom, exercised complete authority in matters concerning the Sikh religion. His order to have the king of the land, the great Maharaja Runjeet Singh, whipped for his violation of Sikh tenants is a firm confirmation of this fact. Many European observers also commented on the supreme authority of the Nihang Singhs;

It is because of its position of authority the term Shiromani (highest of all) is applied to the Budha Dal. In recent times this term has been widely associated with the Shiromani Gurdwara Parbandak Commmitte (SGPC) who were entrusted during the 1920s, during British rule in Punjab, to manage the responsibilities of various Gurdware. In their comparatively short history they have taken many efforts to remove the influence of Budha Dal and its historical legacy from the mainstream of Sikh religion. For decades they have been enlisting the help of courts to try and secure land, property and religious . Since their creation they have sought to bring Budha Dal under its wing by attempting to set up a parallel Budha Dal.

Giani Kirpal Singh, an ex SGPC elected Jathedar of the Akaal Takht notes the historical position of the Nihangs with regards to the Takht Sahibs;

'After the martyrdom of Baba Akali Phula Singh, Baba Hanuman Singh was sworn in Budha Dals next jathedar. After them, Baba Prehlada Singh, Baba Giana Singh served the position of Jathedar of Budha Dal. However, there is a shortage of historical information from their time period. The head priests at Sri Akaal Takht Sahib, Sri Kesgarh Sahib and at Takht Sri Damdama Sahib dressed in the Nihang manner. We are able to tel that the management and control of the Takhts was in the hands of the Jathedar of Budha Dal.Budha Dal looked after all the historic Gurdware in Punjab and paid attention to the preservation of religious traditions and customs. They were also responsible for performing initiation ceremonies and spreading the Sikh Dharam. As the remained always on the move, the general running of the Sikh Takht Sahibs and ensuring that Sikh teachings were properly followed was the responsible of the head priest there.

There is also well decomented service that the senior priests at Takht Sri Hazoor Sahib and Takht Sri Patna Sahib were Nihang Singhs. The Sampradai, traditional orders in the Sikh faith whose instututions existed at the time of Sri Guru Gobind Singh Ji, still recognise the superiority of the Budha Dal. Sant Nahar Singh Nirmala, a leading member of the Nirmal Samprada states.

'Budha Dal is the original Khalsa. Sri Guru Gobind Singh Ji made Baba Binod Singh Ji the head of the Khalsa Panth, after him was Baba Darbara Singh and then Navab Kapoor Singh who named them Budha Dal. They are the Guru Khalsa Panth as ordained by the tenth Guru. Budha Dal is the Shiromani Panth, whenever any head of a Jatha (group) or sampradava was to be selected, it was only Budha Dal who had the power of appointment.'

Although only formally known as Budha Dal since the 1730s, the lineage of Jathedars began ad Baba Binod Singh Ji. Notably Sri Guru Hargobind Sahib Ji had an instrumental role in the formation of Budha Dal and Sri Guru Gobind Singh Ji themselves served as commander of the Khalsa armies. Baba Binod Singh is held as the first Jathedar of Budha Dal as it was he whom Sri Guru Gobind Singh Ji had given the command of the Khalsa Panth to, making him head of the Guru Khalsa Panth. Known as Dal Khalsa to Tat Khalsa and then to Budha Dal in the 1730s, this movement with its unbroken lineage from the Sikh Gurus has been lead by many some of the most famous warrior saints to serve the Khalsa Panth. Baba Budha Ji is seen as the overarching list of. The Jathedars are known as 96 Krori, meaning in charge 960 million Khalsa army which is believed will exist at the time of Khalsa Raj. The term 96 Krori in the Sikh faith is reserved exclusively for the Jathedars Budha Dal who in order have been;

Jathedar Baba Binod Singh Ji

Jathedar Baba Darbara Singh Ji

Jathedar Baba Navab Kapoor Singh Ji

Jathedar Baba Jussa Singh Ji Ahulwala (Sultan Ul Quam)

Jathedar Akali Baba Naina Singh Ji

Jathedar Akali Baba Phula Singh Ji

Jathedar Akali Baba Hanuman Singh Ji

Jathedar Baba Prehlada Singh Ji

Jathedar Baba Giana Singh Ji

Jathedar Baba Teja Singh Ji

Jathedar Baba Sahib Singh Ji Kaladhari

Jathedar Baba Chet Singh Ji

Jathedar Baba Santa Singh Ji

Jathedar Baba Balbir Singh Ji Akali (The Current Jathedar of Budha Dal)

Budha Dal continues today to preach the message of the Guru's and instil martial spirit within the Sikh populace. Budha Dal is contributing towards the society by opening up Schools and other educational institutions and Printing

Press. Its members perform regular religious sermons across India and it is now an established international organisation.

**The Creation of the Taruna Dal from Budha Dal**

Kapur Singh, finding it difficult to manage such a large force centrally, particularly after Darbara Singh's death in 1734, divided the camp into two parts on the basis of age of the Jathedars or group leaders. The elders camp comprising jathas of older leaders such as Sham Singh, Gurbakhsh Singh, Bagh Singh, Gurdial Singh, Sukkha Singh and Kapur Singh which is Buddha (elder) Dal.

The groups of younger Sikhs were called the Taruna (youthful) Dal. The latter was further subdivided into five jathas, each with its own drum and banner. The Buddha Dal too was similarly subdivided after some time. Nawab Kapur Singh remained in overall command of the two Dals which jointly were called the Dal Khalsa. Men were free to join jathas of their choice.

In the old records of the Sikhs we come across only one reference to the strength of a jatha. That is in Ratan Singh Bhangu, Prachin Panth Prakash, which, referring to the fifth jatha of the Taruna Dal commanded by Bir Singh Rarighreta, lists its strength at 1300 horse. From this figure it may be surmised that the jathas broadly comprised 1,300 to 2,000 men each. It was generally agreed that Buddha Dal would remain at Araritsar and manage the shrines, leaving Taruna Dal free for operations in the country.